DEDICATION

Dedicated with sincere thanks to Bill Flavin, Karen Finkenbinder, COL Brett Weigle and the UK Ministry of Defense's Development, Concepts and Doctrine Centre. The encouragement and mentorship provided by all throughout the project is greatly appreciated.

Special acknowledgement to Kim Anderson for her inspiring and inexhaustible patience and support.

FOREWORD

COL John C. Anderson's paper on human security as grand strategy is very timely given the last twelve years of war. As an experienced civil affairs commander and planner, he has a firsthand experience with challenges and complexity that we face. The debate continues over how best to integrate the collective efforts and resources of the Department of Defense, Department of State, other government organizations, as well as other public and private organizations. Game-changing predictions of the future in Global Trends 2030 and Peace Operations 2025 prove that the interagency coordination debate is as salient as ever. This paper explores how the concept of Human Security can perhaps move the interagency debate to the next level. Viewing Human Security as "boundary object" to bridge cultural and process divides between and among disparate organizations is a viable concept deserving of further exploration.

Colonel Anderson's work also proves timely in light of the Army's recent adoption of a seventh warfighting function- Engagement. This paper recognizes that such a human-domain oriented warfighting function could serve to create greater synergy across the respective DoD and DoS domains. In these tighter fiscal environments, it is imperative that we deliver the best value to our Nation which is essentially providing the most security at the lowest cost. In particular, we need to maximize the effectiveness of our engagement in the shaping phase. To this end military and civilian leaders are encouraging creativity and innovation. A closer examination of the merits of the Human Security, wholly commensurate with Theater Security Cooperation and Building Partner Capacity, might provide game-changing strong foundations for a renewed American grand strategy.

Daniel R. Ammerman
Brigadier General
Commander, 353 Civil Affairs Command

ABSTRACT

Dire forecasts of "game-changing" political, social and environmental upheaval over the next thirty years only add to the pessimism generated by constraining fiscal environments and tangible signs, the world over, of a rising China. These same pressures lend urgency to initiatives that seek greater organizational efficiency in the Department of Defense (DOD) and the Department of State (DOS). Efficient organizations alone will not suffice. Only the development of cross-cutting synergies between them can serve and preserve American preeminence and power in a vastly changing world. Such a task requires a game-changing approach. Adopting the human security paradigm as grand strategy can inclusively and powerfully integrate United States Government (USG) functions for international development and building partner capacity. In the process, the versatile human security concept will generate stable foundations for security, governance and rule of law abroad while preserving, and even increasing, American leadership around the globe. Utilizing elements of the Army design methodology and creativity theory, this monograph explores how human security can revolutionize DOD and DOS coordination and, more importantly, action.

ABOUT THE AUTHORS

COLONEL JOHN C. ANDERSON is a USAR AGR officer currently serving as the Deputy Assistant Chief of Staff for Army Reserve Affairs for US Army Central (USARCENT) supporting for the USARCENT Commander all Army Reserve equities and initiatives in the US Central Command (CENTCOM) AOR from Camp Arifjan, Kuwait and Shaw Air Force Base, South Carolina. In previous assignments, COL Anderson commanded the 443d Civil Affairs Battalion at Newport, Rhode Island and served as the Brigade S3 for the 304th Civil Affairs Brigade in Philadelphia. Experienced at the tactical, operational and strategic levels in civil-military operations, Colonel Anderson was among the first Army Reserve Civil Affairs personnel deployed to Afghanistan in Operation Enduring Freedom in March 2002. His other operational deployments include Bosnia, and two deployments to Operation Iraqi Freedom in 2004 and 2008/9. COL Anderson holds a Bachelor of Arts degree in English from The Citadel, an International MBA from the University of South Carolina, and Masters degrees in Security Studies and Strategic Studies from the Kansas State University and the US Army War College respectively. COL Anderson also holds Certificates in Stability, Security and Development in Complex Operations and Rule of Law from the Naval Postgraduate School.

CHANGING THE GAME:
HUMAN SECURITY AS GRAND STRATEGY

Our national security depends on human security —
on preventing and responding to crisis and conflict,
securing democracy, and advancing human rights.
— *Quadrennial Diplomacy and*
Development Review

Stabilisation is a creative process. Not a science.
— *JDP 3-40, Stabilisation:*
The Military Contribution (UK)

INTRODUCTION

Dire forecasts of "game-changing" political, social
and environmental upheaval over the next fifteen years
only add to the pessimism generated by constraining
fiscal environments and tangible signs the world over
of a rising China. These same pressures lend supreme
urgency to initiatives that seek greater organizational
efficiency in the Department of Defense (DoD) and the
Department of State (DoS) respectively. Efficient organizations alone will not suffice, however. Only the
development of cross-cutting synergies among those
organizations can serve and preserve American preeminence and power in a vastly changing world. The
task will require its own game-changing approach.
Adoption of the human security paradigm as grand
strategy can inclusively and powerfully integrate
United States Government (USG) functions for international development, stability operations and build-

1

ing partner capacity. In the process, the versatile human security concept will generate stable foundations for security, governance and rule of law abroad while preserving and even increasing American leadership around the globe. Utilizing elements of the Army design methodology and elements from creativity and organizational theory, this monograph will explore how human security can revolutionize DoD and DoS coordination and more importantly how it would generate powerful action warranting its rise to the level of USG grand strategy.

This paper argues that the foundational work already accomplished toward better military-civilian coordination over the past ten years of stability operations must continue. Progress already achieved can serve as valuable input to full DoS and DoD synchronization operationalized through establishment of a human security framework. The first section offers an explanation of human security with a particular focus on its freedom from want and freedom from fear aspects. Additionally, a brief review of the literature will reveal that the concept shares both proponents who cast it as a potentially powerful concept for development; as well as detractors who claim that the concept's vagueness, expansiveness, and even vulnerability to political manipulation render its utility minimal. The third section employs operational design methodology utilizing the ZIF "Peace Operations 2025" report and the National Intelligence Council's "Alternative Worlds: Global Trends 2030". The fourth section proposes a human security framework for all United States interaction abroad employing creativity and organizational theory in support of the argument. The final section predicts the beneficial grand strategy effect of a human security framework on both national security and power and offers a set of recommendations for further research and suggestions for gradual implementation.

WHAT IS HUMAN SECURITY?

Introduced nearly twenty years ago, the concept of human security is by no means new. Emergence of the concept roughly coincided with the end of the Cold War and the concomitant reevaluation of the international system that included early attempts at envisaging forms of "extended security".[1] Yet, the concept retains a certain newness even today owing to its difficulty in sustaining critical mass momentum necessary for full realization of its potential. Governments reluctant to abandon the established state-centered view of security prove even more hesitant to embrace the more comprehensive individual-centered view of security espoused in the United Nations Development Programme's landmark 1994 Human Development Report. The Human Development Report announced in the opening pages that it would explore "new frontiers" ushering in "preventive diplomacy and preventive development" calling on "all nations to recognize that it is far cheaper and far more humane to act early and to act upstream than to pick up the pieces downstream, to address the root causes of human insecurity rather than its tragic consequences."[2] Assessing security in this manner required an innovative approach that also addressed the multi-faceted nature of those root causes. Rather than focus on building security through strengthening a state's defense apparatus, the preventive aspect of human security flows from its innovative and simultaneous dual focus on individual "freedom from want" and "freedom from fear". In the human security construct, want and fear result from

3

the convergence of multiple vulnerabilities in the environment of the individual.

LITERATURE REVIEW

A growing body of literature exists that embraces Human Security's multi-dimensionality in the search for a viable framework for wider implementation. This work transcends divisive and confrontational debate surrounding the concept's definitional ambiguity and or expansiveness. Instead of writing off human security as an untenable concept, certain schools have emerged that explore its specific aspects. These constructive arguments support moves toward holistic arrangements of human security tenets for facilitation of policy recommendations and formulation. A contributor to *Rethinking Human Security*, Paul Oquist identifies four groups that seek to drive the human security policy agenda.

- *First Group- Developmental Analysts*
  Those seeking to move "beyond narrow national economic growth concepts of development to broader people-centered concepts such as "sustainable human development" and "human security".

- *Second Group- Environmental Analysts and Activists*
  Those emphasizing "interrelations between global governance and the governance necessary in confronting contemporary environmental challenges" while recognizing "save the species as a more productive call than save the planet."

4

- *Third Group- International Relations Analysts*
  Those who have "moved beyond narrow national security concepts based merely on territory to a broader human security concept that is people-centered."

- *Fourth Group- Disaster and Conflict Mitigation and Recovery*
  Those exploring threats of natural disaster and violent conflict, mitigation, relief and recovery.[3]

Indeed, the best possible human security policy agenda and framework would integrate narrative and tangible activity components from each of the four groups. This paper will argue that an integrative comprehensive approach to human security will prove the most effective approach. Most importantly, however, Oquist notes that "effective policy needs more than extra resources and greater political commitment; it also requires a better understanding of global and regional security trends."[4] The following section will go one step further exploring not only global regional security trends but also their contribution, interactions and ultimately predicted impacts far into the future.

UNDERSTANDING THE FUTURE OPERATIONAL ENVIRONMENT

America's future role and contribution to peace and security in the international system will forever remain a function of its own capacity and the evolving complexities of the international system. One approach for estimating the trajectory and magnitude of American leadership in the world of the future involves estimating the future itself—analyzing today those complexities of tomorrow. Decrements in the capacities of today to effectively deal with the complexities of tomorrow should then inform the targeted reshaping or new development of policy, procedures and structure.

Preparing for the future through best predicting it to any measure of accuracy can be considered an ill-structured problem suitable to application of design methodology since that approach encourages "critical thought, innovation and creativity."[5] Producing a successful design will require answering three basic questions that correspond to the three design spaces—operational environment, problem and solution, respectively.[6]

DESIGN SPACES	THREE BASIC DESIGN QUESTIONS
OPERATIONAL ENVIRONMENT	What is the context in which the design will be implemented?
PROBLEM	What problem is the design intended to address?
SOLUTION	How will the design resolve or manage the problem?[7]

The ability afforded by the design methodology to move between and develop the design spaces "iteratively and concurrently allows a coherent understanding to emerge that relates the solution to the problem in the context of the environment." [8] For the purposes of this paper, two scenario based reports will assist in overcoming the challenge of working with a notional future-based operational environment. These reports, the National Intelligence Council's "Alternative Worlds: Global Trends 2030" and the Zentrum für Internationale Friedenseinsätze Center for Peace Operation's "Peace Operations 2025"[9] lend credibility and rigor to our exercise owing not only to their similarity in methodology, verbiage and findings; but also to their common 2012 publication dates.

A systematic analysis of the two futurist reports utilizing the specific steps for working in the three design spaces will mitigate the complexities of the task. Joint Publication 5-0 (JP 5-0), Joint Operations Planning offers an excellent guide to these steps that are engineered for understanding "conceptually the broad solutions for attaining mission accomplishment and to reduce the uncertainty of a complex operational environment."[10] The methodology itself is governed by an organizational learning methodology grounded in the exploration of answers to additional targeted questions related to understanding the strategic direction and operational environment, defining the problem and problem-solving approaches.[11]

DESIGN STEPS	ORGANIZATIONAL LEARNING QUESTIONS
UNDERSTAND THE STRATEGIC DIRECTION	What are the strategic goals to be achieved?
UNDERSTAND THE OPERATIONAL ENVIRONMENT	What is the larger context that will help determine the problem?
DEFINE THE PROBLEM	What problem is the design intended to solve?
OPERATIONAL APPROACH	How will the problem be solved?[12]

JP 5-0 asserts that the strategic guidance "should define what constitutes "victory" or success (ends) and allocate adequate forces and resources (means) to achieve strategic directives" adding that "the President, SecDef, CJCS and CCDRs all promulgate strategic guidance."[13] In the recognition that documents emanating from these sources of authority originate with the President's own guidance for the nation, the most logical starting point for Understanding the Strategic Direction rests squarely on the National Security Strategy.

The most recent National Security Strategy published in May of 2010 serves as both the strategic guidance for this paper as well as an ideal overarching theme complementing the future focus of this paper as it juxtaposes the "The World We Seek" against "The World As It Is."[14] Closing the decrement between "The World As It Is" and "The World We Seek" involves continued progress and maintenance toward supporting and sustaining the enduring national interests. In a section entitled "Strategic Approach," they are listed as follows:

- *The security of the United States, its citizens, and U.S. allies and partners;*

- A strong, innovative, and growing U.S. economy in an open international economic system that promotes opportunity and prosperity;

- *Respect for universal values at home and around the world; and*

- *An international order advanced by U.S. leadership that promotes peace, security, and opportunity through stronger cooperation to meet global challenges.*[15]

Since these interests are enduring, for the purposes of this paper they will encompass "The World We Seek" while the two futurist reports detailed below will serve as a notional, predicted and anticipated "World As It Is". It will be shown that three of these enduring national interests already relate to and can be strengthened by the concept of human security.

ALTERNATIVE WORLDS

"Alternative Worlds 2030" is not the first Global Trends report published by the National Intelligence Council. The reports represent more an iterative process than an event as the authors review the actual unfolding of events in the international system and compare those events with trends predicted in previous Global Trends reports.[16] Although striving for accuracy in prediction, the authors cede that they "do not seek to predict the future---which would be an impossible feat". Rather, the goal involves providing "a framework for thinking about possible futures and their implications."[17] Treating these "possible futures" as a future operational environment reveal sets of unique environmental phenomena termed "Megatrends" and "Game Changers". The "Megatrends" manifest partially already today are predicted to "deepen and become more intertwined producing a more qualitatively different world."[18] In addition to acknowledging that 2030 will be a radically different world, the "Game Changers" are those factors or potentialities that interact with each other to determine the magnitude and impact of the change. Hence, the "Megatrends" are stated and fast approaching as reality while the "Game Changers" are noted with accompanying questions:

MEGATRENDS
Individual Empowerment
The Diffusion of Power
Demographic Patterns
The Growing Nexus of Food, Water, and Energy

GAME CHANGERS
The Crisis Prone Global Economy Will divergences among players with different economic interests and global volatility result in a worldwide economic breakdown and collapse? Or will the development of multiple growth centers lead to increased resiliency in the global economic order?
The Governance Gap Will current governments and international institutions be able to adapt fast enough to harness change or be overwhelmed by it?
The Potential for Increased Conflict Will rapid changes and shifts in power lead to more intrastate and interstate conflicts?
Wider Scope of Regional Instability Will regional spillover, especially in the Middle East and South Asia cause global instability?
The Impact of New Technologies Will technological breakthroughs be developed in time to boost economic productivity and solve the problems caused by the strain on natural resources and climate change as well as chronic disease, aging populations, and rapid urbanization.
The Role of the United States Will the US be able to work with new partners to reinvent the international system, carving out new roles and an expanded world order.

The Megatrends and Game Changers form the basis of the report's four alternative worlds coined Stalled Engines, Fusion, Gini-Out-of-the-Bottle, and Nonstate World.[19] As alluded to above, the deviating impacts of the Megatrends and the Game Changers account for the variations in the Alternative Worlds. Although the Alternative Worlds vary on scales of most optimistic to very pessimistic, change in the historic status quo, an increase in regional conflict and growing resource constraints (due to various factors) all serve as the common themes.

PEACE OPERATIONS 2025

Invariably, no matter how robust or successful USG development and partner capacity building figures over the next three decades, outbreaks of conflict necessitating intervention will undoubtedly occur. Anticipating this reality, the ZIF Peace Operations 2025 report examines the impact of "key factor projections" on the future of peace operations itself.[20] Using scenarios to distinguish among factors "whose development can be influenced and those that must be accepted as given," Peace Operations aims to stimulate thinking on "which factors could truly change the game."[21]

Similarly structured through identification of trends, game changers, and scenario future worlds; Peace Operations 2025 also further employs a notion of supply and demand. Supply refers to capacity and willingness for interventions and peacekeeping and contrasts those levels with demand viewed as the magnitude of instability and conflict in 2025. The most striking aspect of Peace Operations 2025 when analyzed alongside Global Trends 2030: Alternative Worlds, is the full agreement or close intersections on both the future drivers of conflict in the international system and the potentials for greater cooperation. They are:

KEY FACTOR PROJECTIONS
National Interest versus Global Interdependence
State of the Global Economy
Economic and Political Power Shifts
Norms and Values
Evolution of International Organizations
State Fragility
Organized Crime
Resource Scarcity
Migration, Refugees and Diasporas
New Technologies
New Media
Private Security Companies
Demographics
Climate Change

Peace Operations 2025's corollary to Global Trend 2030s Alternative Worlds is a set of four "scenarios." The authors justify plausibility of the scenarios thirteen years in the future by highlighting the unprecedented developments in peacekeeping over the past thirteen years[22] conceding that peacekeeping operations is so mutable that the "most daring scenario would probably be one in which things stay just the way they are."[23]

TOWARD A HUMAN SECURITY FRAMEWORK

Considering the alternative worlds and the future supply and demand for interventions, this paper asks the following research question. What should the United States do to prepare for global leadership in a world envisioned by "Global Trends: Alternative Worlds" and "Peace Operations 2025?" In short, if the "World as It Is" of the National Security were the predicted world of the futurist reports; how could the United States best support its enduring national interests to arrive at "The World We Seek?" Here the Problem Framing portion of design methodology dictates that planners Identify the Problem. The inputs from this step prove key in the construction of the output- a Problem Statement around which an Operational Approach can be designed to solve the problem.

According to JP 5-0, defining the problem consists of a "review of the tendencies and potentials of all concerned actors" coupled with "identifying tensions among the existing conditions and the desired end state."[24] Drawing on the analysis of the futurist reports for the problem identification data, three key questions emerge. First, common to most national security problems, identification of the problem relates to how well the United States currently brings all elements of national power to bear on conflict and development in "The World As It Is." Additionally, the problem relates to how the employment of the elements of national power could result in sustainable trajectories for peace, democracy and development in engagements in the predicted international system. The third problem relates to cost-effectiveness in a fiscally constrained environment wherein peace and development initiatives compete with costs to maintain peerless military power. The design methodology advocates the incorporation of these cascading, interconnected problems into a single all-encompassing Problem Statement. The following proposed Problem Statement therefore seeks to "articulate how the operational variables[25] can be expected to resist or facilitate transformation and how inertia in the operational environment can be leveraged to ensure the desired conditions are achieved":[26]

> Over the next fifteen years, how can the United States maintain its influence and power in a world characterized by a lack of hegemonic powers but an increase in nations nonetheless wielding regional influence while contending with a growing world middle class that highlights income disparities and causes a shifting of power from nation states to networks and individuals while remaining a peerless military power?

The most adequate answer to such a complex multi-dimensional question must necessarily address its multiple facets. Since any one element of national power is unlikely to solve the problem as stated in total, only a framework that harnesses all elements of national power to the greatest synergistic and cost-efficient effect could possibly prove viable. It is assumed that the cost effectiveness of the approach operant on other variables in the problem statement would preserve the economic wherewithal to maintain peerless military power status. A human security approach to USG engagement around the world carries such potential, increasing in efficiency especially over the long term.

As noted in the literature review above some scholars assert that human security's viability for encompassing a policy and implementation framework remains untapped. In the first annual meeting of the directors of peace research and training institutions for the United Nations Education Scientific and Cultural Organization (UNESCO) in November of 2000, the directors asserted that the maturation and development of the concept should not detract from its potential to both understand the environment and mobilize responses.[27] In the meeting themed "What agenda for human security in the twenty-first century?" the participants concluded the following:

> (Human security is) a paradigm in the making for ensuring both a better knowledge of the rapidly evolving large-scale risks and threats that can have a major impact on individuals and populations and a strengthened mobilization of a wide-array of actors actually involved in participative policy formulation in the various fields it encompasses. [28]

Even if no agreement exists among scholars and experts on the nature of the evolving threats or the exact human security stances and initiatives that could or should be enshrined in policy, a good first step calls for recognizing the accrual of advantages derived from a holistic integrated approach "compared to traditional policy frameworks" [29]

Oquist cites eight advantages that would accrue if policies were analyzed through an integrated holistic human security policy framework. They are:

- It strengthens policy, reduces risks and enhances opportunities across all policy spheres and at all levels from the species to the individual level.

- It allows for systematic comparisons by establishing an integrated prioritization of human security policy across all policy spheres and potentially at different policy levels.

- It facilitates resource allocation through comprehensive analysis and prioritization across all policy spheres and at different policy levels.

- It creates the possibility of integrated policy actions at different levels and in different spheres in the operational, as well as the planning, stages.

- It permits greater sensitivities to trade-offs between policy priorities.

- It focuses attention on how much to invest in low-risk policy contingencies that would have catastrophic consequences.

- It advances human security through establishing a network of interconnected formal and institutional networks to bring together key decision makers.

- It reaffirms that "one size fits all" policies do not work and that the human security framework requires case-based analysis that includes policy, institutional and cultural dimensions.[30]

Reverse engineering the benefits above, it might be concluded that without an overarching narrative, hierarchical, multi-level organizations might suffer from compartmentalized structures and accompanying policies that compromise internal efficiency as well as compound difficulties in lateral coordination with like-structured organizations. Harnessing such organizations toward common goals proves problematic unless all the organizations already possess similar goals when working toward a common goal.

The human security concept possesses the capacity for simultaneously serving as the similar goal and the common language vertically within organizations and horizontally among them. Adoption of the human security concept in the USG carries enormous potential for securing the enduring national interests as the world trends toward any one of the stated scenario worlds out to 2030. United States leadership in the world of the future will require more than mere codification of coordination mechanisms among the instruments of national power. It will become imperative that the organizations representing the instruments of national power share similar goals referenced through a common operational language.

Writing in "Human Security from Paradigm Shift to Operationalization: Job Description for a Human Security Worker", Marlies Glasius states that human security serves as a "bridging concept" treating 'formerly' realistic concerns for the security of one's own polity and formerly 'ethical' concerns for human beings elsewhere as inseparable."[31] Glasius drew on the works of Des Gasper further explaining that the bridging function of the human security concept originates from its status as a boundary object. Gasper remarked that boundary objects exist as concepts "malleable enough to be used by diverse parties, while robust enough to keep sufficient shared meaning across (a) range of users."[32] The notion of a boundary object proves key when considering the optimum coordination of diverse entities each possessed of its own unique organizational missions, mandates and cultures. The history of the term can be traced to interdisciplinary collaborators, sociologist Susan Leigh Star and philosopher James R. Griesemer, who published a 1989 article describing it thus:

> Boundary objects are objects which are both plastic enough to adapt to local needs and constraints of the several parties employing them, yet robust enough to maintain a common identity across sites. They are weakly structured in common use, and become strongly structured in individual-site use. They may be abstract or concrete. They have different meanings in different social worlds but their structure is common enough to more than one world to make them recognizable, a means of translation. The creation and management of boundary objects is key in developing and maintaining coherence across intersecting social worlds.[33]

Considering human security as a boundary object in the ways described above both strengthens arguments for and weakens arguments against its use as a viable framework mechanism. Adhering to the criteria in this definition, one could imagine the possibilities and understand why some scholars prize the "fluidity of the concept, the tug-of-war over its true meaning, that allows for critical reflection on various elements on government policy."[34]

Yet, the true operationalization requires then the adoption of a human security approach across multiple disciplines, departments and organizations. This paper identifies four challenges to operationalization of human security in the USG. Determining what specific aspects of a broader human security concept fit current organizational mandates and visions represent the first challenge. In a set of organizations, a second and even larger challenge remains organizational first adoption of human security to anchor the boundary object aspect. The third challenge involves ensuring that an overarching vision or policy grounds and binds the disparate organizations together under an umbrella of human security. The final and most difficult challenge proves to be a uniquely human one. Despite the vast amount of talent in the DoS and DoD, specialization driven by human nature holds sway over beneficial full and integrated collaboration. Author of *Creativity: Flow and the Psychology of Discovery and Invention*, Mihály Csíkszentmihályi states this aspect best writing:

> They love to make connections with adjacent areas of knowledge. They tend to be—in principle—caring and sensitive. Yet the demands of their role inevitably push them toward specialization and selfishness. Of the many paradoxes of creativity, this is perhaps the most difficult to avoid.[35]

The USG cannot allow any barriers to creativity stifle its power and prestige moving toward a future encompassing the worlds described as highly possible over the next fifteen years.

Both the DoS and the DoD have achieved progress in meeting the first two challenges. Meeting the third challenge will require incorporation of human security in a vigorous reaiming of the National Security Strategy. Similarly, obstacles to overcoming the fourth challenge involving specialization will erode once human security becomes USG policy. Cascading out of a new National Security Strategy, human security holds the power to connect national security policy to the DoS's QDDR through to the military's stability operations doctrine. In this case, creative minds in the diplomacy, development and defense domains will merge creating a new domain of human security for the USG. Fortunately, precedent exists for detailed involvement in interagency coordination in general and stability operations in particular at the President of the United States (POTUS) level. Fortunately, respective organizational cultures at both the DoS and DoD are evolving slowing over time in response to POTUS directives.

The DoS embraced human security in the publication of the first ever Quadrennial Diplomacy and Development Review (QDDR) in 2010. The inclusion of human security in the report remains overshadowed by the groundbreaking aspect of its very publication, however. The impetus for the construction and publication of the QDDR lies in the National Security Presidential Directive 44 (NSPD-44) issued by President George W. Bush in 2005. Ultimately, the directive addressed a growing interagency recognition of the need to close an obvious stability operations gap. For the DoS, the gap which came to the fore during protracted stability operations in Iraq and Afghanistan concerned the absence of civilian policy and procedure to support development work in tenuous, non-permissive and even dangerous environments which hampered Phase IV efficiency. There existed no stability operations corollary lying on the scale between the relief work conducted by the Office of Foreign Disaster Assistance's (OFDA) and development work conducted by the United States Agency for International Development (USAID).[36]

In keeping with much post – 911 legislation and reform, the NSPD-44 served as yet more USG recognition of the dangers emanating from failed-states and the government's resolve and commitment to meet those challenges head-on. The directive states that a "focal point" is needed and that the "Secretary of State shall coordinate and lead integrated United States Government efforts involving all U.S. Departments and Agencies with relevant capabilities to prepare, plan for and conduct stabilization and reconstruction activities," including coordinating "such efforts with the Secretary of Defense to ensure harmonization with any planned or ongoing U.S. military operations across the spectrum of conflict."[37] In combination with Department of Defense Directive 3000.05, released ten days earlier, which ordered that "stability operations are a core US military mission that the DoD should be prepared to conduct and support,"[38] the USG seemed poised to operationalize stability and reconstruction through policy-directed integration of the diplomatic and military instruments of national power. Had the game really changed?

Events on the ground in 2006-7 in Iraq revealed that the conduct of stability operations do not necessarily preclude devolvement of the situation on the ground into insurgency and a subsequent requirement for counter-insurgency operations (COIN). The violent insurgency refocused the growing the stability operations doctrinal debate toward a COIN-centric relook and eventual long-overdue rewriting of counter-insurgency doctrine. Authored and championed by GEN David Petraeus, FM 3-24 Counterinsurgency changed the mindset from one of fighting insurgents to that of securing the population- a strategy resourced by increased troop deployments in what became known as the Surge. Rather than close the discussion here in recognition that the Surge succeeded, it is useful to re-examine the pre-Surge debate around the time of the FM 3-24's publication.

Many concluded that the US faced an intractable situation in Iraq and therefore remained skeptical that any strategy to include a revamped COIN strategy would solve the problem. Most clamored for improved interagency coordination citing it key to stabilizing Iraq while others blamed the lack of interagency coordination itself for the growing insurgency. Writing in Military Review, Sarah Sewall's comments illustrate those contemporary sentiments perfectly stating:

> It's become vogue to cite a lack of interagency cooperation and civilian capacity in Iraq and beyond, yet the prior failing is conceptual. It's difficult to codify process or build capacity in the absence of a universal doctrinal framework. More narrowly, even the extant military doctrine is on shaky ground when broader governmental assumptions, principles and requirements remain unknown or ad hoc. Creating a common understanding of insurgency and the demands for defeating it remain a core challenge for the nation.[39]

Sewall's points ring wholly cogent. Did the US apply so much emphasis and progress toward generating and operationalizing stability operations doctrine only to discover it possibly irrelevant and obsolete in the ongoing bloody case study of Iraq? Or, was the problem a result of a stability operations doctrine unanchored in policy? Yet, Sewall is not indicting stability operations doctrine as a failed concept. Rather, she is pointing out that doctrine cannot serve as policy no more than it can serve without an overarching policy. As author of the Introduction to the University of Chicago Press edition of FM 3-24, Sewall even more candidly elucidated the point, stating:

The field manual invites the nation's political leaders to take responsibility for counterinsurgency. In a sense, the doctrine was written by the wrong people. Perhaps more accurately it emerged of necessity from the wrong end of the COIN equation. Because counterinsurgency is predominately political, military doctrine should flow from a larger strategic framework. But political leaders have failed to find a compelling one. Since the armed forces are carrying almost the entire burden in Iraq, it is unsurprising that they felt compelled to tackle the problem anyway. But the doctrine is a moon without a planet to orbit.[40]

The success of the Surge does not diminish Sewall's lament above. Conversely, the success of the Surge and Sewall's comments both serve the argument for an overarching human security framework enshrined in USG policy. To borrow from Sewall's celestial analogy, the DoS policy and DoD doctrinal moons require a USG human security strategy "planet" around which to orbit.

A closer examination of human security as referenced in the QDDR and other US and partner nation government documents prove its growing mention can serve as foundation for its becoming a boundary object- achieving the long sought interagency coordination through human security and in service to its potential as US grand strategy.

The following survey though DoS policy and DoD doctrine citing human security reveals its synergistic promise not only between the DOS and other departments, namely the DoD; but also with the greater world-wide development and peace-building community at large. Human security's move away from its existence as a United Nations project-concept (surrounded by an attendant academic debate) and into actionable government and non-governmental initiatives is afoot and gaining momentum. The USG must embrace human security as the overarching framework for the development and stability operations in order to lead in the non-hegemonic world of the future.

No disagreement regarding vast changes on the horizon in the international system exists between the QDDR and the futurist documents highlighted above. The QDDR states that "trend lines indicate the forces of political instability and natural disasters will increase and diversify over the next decade in areas critical to our national security and prosperity."[41] Meeting the challenges will require conflict and crises prevention, and response methodologies that the QDDR admits "previously were not integrated and focused on the problem in a sustained way."[42] The QDDR juxtaposes its indictment of the DoS failures in the past with a call to action comprising seven key initiatives born of lessons learned both from past successes and failures. They are:

- *Adopt a lead-agency approach between State and USAID based on clear lines of authority, a complimentary division of labor, joint structures and systems, and standing agreements with other agencies;*

- *Bring together a cadre of personnel experienced in this discipline within a new bureau, fill out a standing interagency response corps that can deploy quickly and flexibly in the field, and provide broader training for diplomats, civil servants, and development professionals;*

- *Develop a single planning process for conflict prevention and resolution, sustainable governance, and security assistance in fragile states, including planning to address potential intended consequences of our assistance and operations;*

- **Develop standing guidance and an international operational response framework to provide crisis and conflict prevention and response that is not dependent on individual embassies;**

- **Create new ways and frameworks for working with the military to prevent and resolve conflict, counter insurgencies and illicit actors, and create safe, secure environments for local populations;**

- **Coordinate and integrate assistance to foreign militaries, civilian police, internal security institutions, and justice sector institutions to promote comprehensive and sustainable security and justice sector reform; and**

- **Strengthen our capacity to anticipate crisis, conflict, and potential mass atrocities and raise awareness of emerging governance problems.** [43]

It can be argued that all of these QDDR initiatives either seek to establish those synergies characteristic of a human security framework espoused by Oquist and mentioned above (those in italics) or directly relate to human security in action (those in bold).

The true landmark aspect of the QDDR lies in its focus on human security. The DoS makes the case for human security clear in a section entitled, "Adapting to the Diplomatic Landscape of the 21st Century" wherein it asserts that to give "human security issues the priority they demand, the existing Under Secretary for Democracy and Global Affairs will be reorganized into an Under Secretary for Civilian Security, Democracy, and Human Rights."[44] The document goes on to describe the referenced human security issues in the "State Department's mandate". They are listed as:

- preventing and responding to conflict and crisis;

- managing refugee and humanitarian crises, and our support for major international organizations involved in aid to conflict affected populations;

- advancing human rights and democratic values; and

- countering the convergence of transnational threats such as the threat of narcotics, transnational crime, and insurgency.[45]

The military is making progress as well on the concept of human security. The graph below referred to as "Elements of a Stable State" from Joint Publication 3-07 (published shortly after the QDDR) is supported by the following explanation:

the primary military contribution to stabilization is to protect and defend the population, facilitating the personal security of the people and, thus, creating a platform for political, economic, and human security.[46]

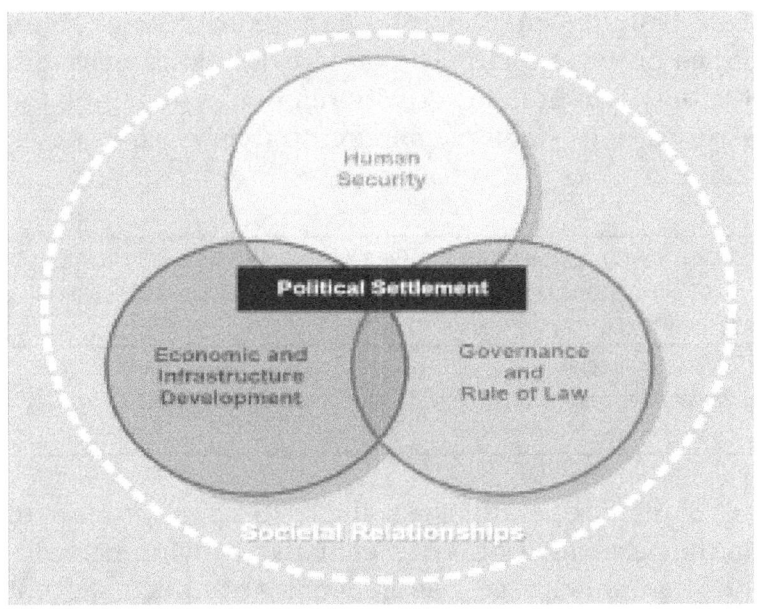

Although this explanation somewhat deviates from the understanding that political security and economic security are part of human security and not separate from it; the fact that the JP 3-07 mentions human security twenty times is encouraging (especially compared to nine mentions in the QDDR). The same cannot be said for the Army's own stability operations manuals, although there does exist some progress.

The much anticipated Field Manual 3-07 published in October of 2008 contained no mention of human security. The Army's new Army Doctrine Publication (ADP) for stability operations, ADP 3-07, mentions only "human development" and "human dimension"; although it mentions theses terms numerous times. This lack of including or mirroring human security from the Joint Publication by cascading it down into the ADP is discouraging. Interestingly however, the ADP 3-07's more thorough companion reference document, Army Doctrine Reference Publication (ADRP)

3-07 Stability, mentions human security twice (both times on page 3-20). The table below cites verbatim the only two human security references in among the Army's new stability manuals published in August 2012.

An underlying objective for many of the supporting tasks is to protect civilians from threats not necessarily related to conflict. Sometimes other **human security** threats may be paramount.
The third conceptual line, the Protection of Civilians from **Human Security** Threats, is less tied to UN origins and subsumes the expanded list issues identified above.

Stability operations are likely to figure prominent in the possible futures depicted above owing especially to an anticipated rise in regional conflict. Recent history is useful to inform what should be the Army position on human security. Iraq is the shining example for all time for why the Army should embrace human security in stability operations. The success of the Surge in Iraq can attributed to a shift from a state-security centric mission (fighting an insurgency on behalf of the Host Nation) to a human security centric mission wherein securing the population held primacy –and succeeded. Who would dare say the Surge did not work? Who did not think Iraq an intractable conflict in 2006? The Surge worked because it was based on providing the population enough "freedom from fear" to gain space for stability.[47] Some would argue that the Surge worked because it was a COIN operation. Yet, would there ever have been an insurgency if human security principles had informed Phase IV planning for Iraq in 2003? Population centric aspects of COIN are also synonymous with human security.

The graph below envisions a human security domain for the USG. The Stability Sectors and Stability Tasks are similar yet distinct residing in the respective DoS and DoD domains. The collaboration occurs at the interstitial nodes in the human security boundary object area. Best practices occur and develop around these interstitial nodes. Most importantly, actions at these nodes will come to represent linkages to DoS efforts at Host Nation federal and provincial levels to DoD levels at province and below. Some collaboration among the two organizations is already ongoing in development at these interstitial nodes. The growing body of literature and recognition of the import of Security Sector Reform (SSR) is a ready example. The Army's exploration of a 7th Warfighting Function is key to success of this framework. Upon adoption, the Human Domain Warfighting function would reside in the Army domain ---in effect serving as boundary object in its own right to human security based stability operations and the Army institution at large. The cross linkages between all the interstitial nodes represent the power of human security and the prudence of working on all tasks and sectors simultaneously in DoS and DoD collaboration.

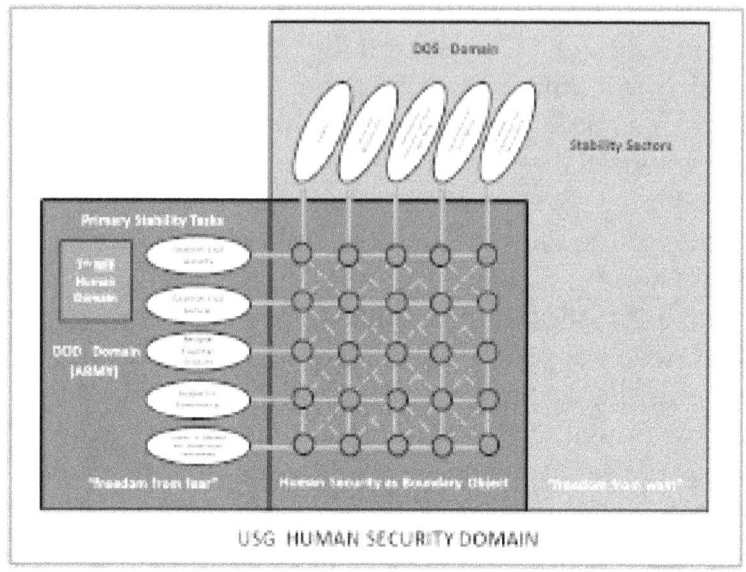

GRAND STRATEGY ASPECTS OF A
HUMAN SECURITY DOMAIN

The eminent strategist Colin Gray reminds prac-
titioners of the tedium involved in the selection and
implementation of a grand strategy when he states;
"between the elevated heights of ideology and policy,
on the one hand, and expert military behaviour, on
the other, there is the difficult realm of strategy, especially grand strategy."[48] Recognizing the terms' fre-
quent employment "in such a way that it is not clear
whether the author means military strategy or grand
strategy", Gray asserts that "grand strategy refers to
the purposeful employment of all of the assets of a
state, not only to the use of the military instrument." [49]
Colin Gray is in good company on the topic of grand
strategy with B. H. Liddell Hart who himself even
proves more useful than Clausewitz here.

Proponent of the indirect approach, Hart both defined the grand strategy concept and illuminated its absolute utility in his classic treatise *Strategy*. In a section entitled "Higher, or Grand Strategy," he wrote:

> As tactics is an application of strategy on a lower plane, so strategy is an application on a lower plane of "grand strategy". While practically synonymous with the policy which guides the conduct of war, as distinct from the more fundamental policy which should govern its object, the term "grand strategy" serves to bring out the sense of "policy in execution". For the role of grand strategy-higher strategy- is to co-ordinate and direct all the resources of a nation, or band of nations, towards the attainment of the political object of war- the goal defined by fundamental policy.

> Grand strategy should both calculate and develop the economic resources and man-power of nations in order to sustain the fighting services. Also the moral resources- for to foster the people's willing spirit is often as important as to possess the more concrete forms of power. Grand strategy, too, should regulate the distribution of power between the several services, and between the services and industry. Moreover, fighting power is but one of the instruments of grand strategy-which should take account of and apply the power of financial pressure, and, not least of ethical pressure, to weaken the opponents will to resist, as well as augmenting moral strength.

> Furthermore, while the horizon of strategy is bounded by the war, grand strategy looks beyond the war to the subsequent peace. It should not only combine the various instruments, but so regulate their use as to avoid damage to the future of peace- for its security and prosperity. The sorry state of peace, for both sides, that has followed most wars can be traced to the fact that, unlike strategy, the realm of grand strategy is for

the most part terra incognita- still awaiting exploration and understanding.[50]

Readers no doubt recognize several of Hart's iconic quotes embedded in the above narrative. Reading the text intact illuminates the force of Hart's argument for a grand strategy- its close relationship yet primacy over strategy. Hart reveals that grand strategy is more than merely the coordination of the Diplomatic, Informational, Military and Economic (DIME) instruments of national power applied in a single event, situation or scenario. Rather, grand strategy involves the sustained coordination of those elements over time (running in the background, yet out front in purpose) across the set of all possible events, situations and scenarios in time and space involving the nation.

Fully realizing human security's potential for serving and preserving American prestige and power in the mold of a grand strategy will require creativity. Codification of human security across a growing body of government documents will not suffice. Through creative intra and inter-departmental collaboration, the human security concept must become a domain within the USG. Domains figure prominently in the instructive literature of creativity theorist Csíkszentmihályi who subscribes to a systems model of creative processes. According to Csíkszentmihályi, "creativity can be observed only in the interrelations of a system made up of three main parts"; domains, fields and individuals.[51] The notion of the field is key to the operationalization of any concept since the field consists of those "individuals who act as gatekeepers to the domain" and whose job it is to "decide whether a new idea or product should be included in the domain." [52] So, it could be argued that although key individuals already recognize the import of human security to national security policy and practice, gatekeepers remain who (either unaware or unconvinced) have not allowed its full elevation to domain status in the USG.

The established domains of stability operations and development are related to human security and already exist in the DoD and the DoS respectively. Csíkszentmihályi points out that "occasionally creativity involves the establishment of a new domain."[53] Both departments' activities encompass elements of strategy. Grand strategy involves combinations, however. Some even view the Diplomacy, Development and Defense (3D) construct facilitated by the Whole of Government approach as the long sought US grand strategy.[54] If 3D and the Whole of Government approach were energized through human security principles, 3D has a solid chance of becoming a part of that long sought US grand strategy.

In a landmark organization theory work entitled "Exploration and Exploitation in Organizational Learning", James D. March warned of the dangers stemming from an organizational imbalance between continued exploitation of core competencies at the expense of exploration. March states that "maintaining an appropriate balance between exploration and exploitation is a primary factor in system survival and prosperity...adding that, "adaptive processes, by refining exploitation more rapidly than exploration are likely to become effective in the short run but self-destructive in the long run."[55] In short, the neither the DoS nor the DoD (the Army in particular) can afford to not innovate on all fronts.

RECOMMENDATIONS FOR IMPLEMENTATION AND FURTHER RESEARCH

The next version of the National Security Strategy should express USG support for the concept of human security. There is currently no mention of human security by name although the spirit of the document is awash in human security principles. If the National Security Strategy mentioned human security, the process would be set in motion for its cascading thorough a wide array of government publications thus sanctioning operationalization throughout the USG at the highest levels.

As alluded to above, the Army should embrace human security and codify that support in its stability operations literature. Much of the Army's work involves human security already. Inclusion in the documentation is safe—it will not "dull the sword." Modeling the ADP 3-07 *Stability* after the UK JDP 3-40 would lead to great strides in fostering interagency collaboration and understanding.

Concensus-building and cooperative ventures stand better chances of success when underpinned by shared norms and values. Peace Operations 2025 view "intangible factors" such as norms and values complementing and or competing with the "harder realities of economic and political power" in the future asserting that the "prospects for multilateral action are much better than in one dominated by ethnic, national, social or religious identities and zero-sum competition."[56] Human security principles can and should serve as the norms and values defining American involvement in multilateral peace building operations and initiatives. The relative hope or gloom depicted in the Peace Operations 2025 rises and falls on the issue of shared norms and values. In order to secure the better scenarios for the US, the nation must begin leading as a strong voice and proponent for human security. US adoption of human security can also accelerate and harmonize a predicted increase in so-called "norm-entrepreneurs" or benevolent non-state actors.[57]

Based on a longer timeline than other immediate security programs, human security is right for incorporation into BPC initiatives. Former Secretary of Defense Robert Gates noted that the US must embrace soft power since "over the long term [it] cannot kill or capture its way to victory."[58] Grounded in the "by, with and through" methodology, BPC envisions increasing the proportion of producers of security over consumers of security. Opportunities to convey the iron-clad logic of human security during BPC engagements would surely figure among the most inexpensive and cost effective initiatives ever undertaken by the US government. Spreading of the human security concept during BPC training engagements carries no risk of transmitting American ethno-centric attitudes. American ideals and the human security concept are coterminous. Yet, a 266 page RAND report published in 2010 entitled "Developing an Army Strategy for Building Partner Capacity for Stability Operations" contains no mention of human security.

The nation must not allow the hard won seasoning of its Civil Affairs force to stagnate. The Army's Civil Affairs force (honed sharp through ten years of work up close with indigenous populations and structures) represents the "human security workers" that Glasius refers to in her article. Civil Affairs forces are armed --exactly part of the profile she mentions that "human security workers" should meet. Why could the USG not explore joint-interagency missions deploying Civil Affairs forces alongside DoS personnel in effect operationalizing some of the QDDRs human intiatives?

CONCLUSION

A grand strategy for the USG informed through a state-centric approach will unlikely prove most optimal in a world wherein the game is changing. The future challenges brought on by rising self-empowerment, growing regional structures (and regional conflict), and emerging focus on norms and values envisioned in the alternative worlds and scenarios alone negate the efficacy of state-centric approaches to grand strategy. The alternative worlds and scenarios represented in the creative and ground-breaking work of "Peace Operations 2025" and "Global Trends: 2030 Alternative Worlds" provide an excellent notional operational environment for utilizing operational design in exploring approaches to USG grand strategy over the next fifteen years.

This paper argues that a grand strategy founded on the dual "freedom from fear" and "freedom from want" aspects of human security can reflexively operationalize internal USG collaboration resulting in increased efficiency in engagements with states, non-state actors and populations at large. A human security approach directs focus and actions on the trends (emerging at both sub-regional and sub-national levels) that distress individual lives and impede opportunity. These phenomena ultimately effect regional and national security for the governing bodies and structures of which those populations are a part.

In March's organizational theory terms, over focus on military "hard power" supremacy in response to any potential rising peer challengers is exploitation — in this context dangerous and counterproductive to the realization of a grand strategy. Conversely, continued exploitation of military competencies complemented with exploration of "soft power" through adoption of human security offers enormous potential for the preservation of American preeminence and power over the next fifteen years. Human security now appears in some USG policy and doctrine. The USG must continue to develop human security as a domain moving toward its full adoption as a component of grand strategy-- especially considering that the game is changing.

ENDNOTES

1. Emma Rothschild, "What is Security" Daedalus, 124:3, 53-98. Rothschild notes four main forms comprising the concept of the extension of security; extended downwards from the security of nations to the security of groups and individuals, extended upwards from the security of nations to the security of the international system, extended horizontally to the sorts of security that are in question – from the military to political, economic, social, environmental or human security, and finally the extension of the political responsibility for extending security which is "diffused in all directions from nation states, including upwards to international institutions, downwards to regional or local government and sideways to non-governmental organizations to public opinion and the press, and the abstract forces of nature or of the market."

2. United Nations Development Programme (UNDP), Human Development Report 1994 (New York: Oxford University Press, 1994), iii.

3. Paul Oquist. "Basic Elements of a Policy Framework for Human Security," in Rethinking Human Security eds. Moufida Goucha and John Crowley (Chichester, UK Wiley-Blackwell and UNESCO, 2008)110-111.

4. Oquist, "Basic Elements of a Policy Framework for Human Security," 110.

5. Stefan J. Banach and Alex Ryan, "The Art of Design: A Design Methodology," Military Review (2009): 105.

6. *Ibid.*, 109.

7. *Ibid.*

8. *Ibid.*

9. The ZIF website, *(http://www.zif-berlin.org/en/),* states: "The Center for International Peace Operations (ZIF) is Germany's central point of reference for civilian expertise. On behalf of the Federal Government of Germany and the Bundestag, ZIF recruits and trains German civilian personnel for international peace operations and election observation missions and offers information and advice to national and international decision makers."

10. U.S. Joint Chiefs of Staff, Joint Operation Planning, Joint Publication 5-0 (Washington, DC: U.S. Joint Chiefs of Staff, August 11, 2011), III-2.

11. *Ibid*, III-7.

12. *Ibid.*

13. *Ibid.*

14. National Security Strategy, The White House, Washington, DC, May 2010, 1.

15. National Security Strategy, 7.

16. In an introductory letter accompanying Global Trends 2030, The Chairman of the National Intelligence Committee notes several innovations in this particular report. He cites: a thorough review of the past four Global Trends reports, the sponsoring of a public blog on the report's key themes, conduct of meetings in twenty different countries on the draft with participants ranging

from government, business, universities and think tanks, and expanded coverage on disruptive technologies obtained through participation and involvement of major research laboratories.

17. National Intelligence Council, "Global Trends 2030: Alternative Worlds". (Washington, DC: Office of the Director of National Intelligence) 2012, *http://www.dni.gov/nic/globaltrends. i.*

18. *Ibid*, 8.

19. *Ibid*, 113.

20. Tobias von Gienanth, Wibke Hansen and Stefan Köppe, Peace Operations 2025, (Berlin: Center for International Peace Operations (ZIF)), 2012. *http://www.zif/berlin.org/fileadmin/uploads/ analyse/dokumente /veroeffentlichungen/ZIF_Peace_Operations_2025. pdf,* 4.

21. *Ibid*.

22. The authors note on page 9, "At the time of writing, 2025 is less than thirteen years away – in many ways a short time span. However, looking back at the past thirteen years in peacekeeping gives an idea of the degree of change that can occur during such a time period. In 1999, the UN launched its first ever missions with a broad executive mandate – in Kosovo and East Timor. This also marked the real beginning of state-building as a part of peace operations. That same time period saw the evolution of new norms such as the Responsibility to Protect (R2P), NATO's first use of Article Five in response to 9/11, the deployment of the first EU mission, the first AU mission, and the first hybrid mission. UN personnel in peace operations for the first time exceeded the 100,000 mark and, with peacekeepers on the ground, three new states emerged during this period: Kosovo, Timor-Leste and South Sudan."

23. Tobias von Gienanth, Peace Operations 2025, 9.

24. Joint Chiefs of Staff, Joint Operations Planning, III-12.

25. For the purposes of this paper, the operational variables are the Megatrends, Game Changers and Key Factor Projections in Peace Operations 2025 and Global Trends 2030: Alternative Worlds.

26. Joint Chiefs of Staff, Joint Operations Planning, III-12.

27. The "What We Are" portion of the UNESCO website states that the organization "works to create the conditions for dialogue among civilizations, cultures and peoples, based upon respect for commonly shared values. It is through this dialogue that the world can achieve global visions of sustainable development encompassing observance of human rights, mutual respect and the alleviation of poverty, all of which are at the heart of UNESCO'S mission and activities." The organization works towards these above stated goals through five major program areas: Education, Natural Sciences, Social and Human Sciences, Culture and Communication and Information. *http://www.unesco.org/new/en/*

28. Pierre Sane. "Rethinking Human Security," in Rethinking Human Security eds. Moufida Goucha and John Crowley (Chichester, UK Wiley-Blackwell and UNESCO, 2008) 6.

29. Oquist, "Basic Elements of a Policy Framework for Human Security," 112.

30. *Ibid.*

31. Marlies Glasius, "Human Security from Paradigm Shift to Operationalization: Job Description for a Human Security Worker," Security Dialogue 39, no. 5 (2008), 39.

32. Des Gasper, "Securing Humanity: Situating 'Human Security' as Concept and Discourse", Journal of Human Development 6(2)(2005): 221–245. quoted in Marlies Glasius, "Human Security from Paradigm Shift to Operationalization: Job Description for a Human Security Worker," Security Dialogue 39, no. 5 (2008), 39.

33. Susan Leigh Star, and James R. Griesemer. "Institutional ecology,translations' and boundary objects: Amateurs and professionals in Berkeley's Museum of Vertebrate Zoology, 1907-39." Social Studies of Science 19, no. 3 (1989): 387-420.

34. Glasius, "Human Security from Paradigm Shift to Operationalization: Job Description for a Human Security Worker," 45.

35. Mihály Csíkszentmihályi, Creativity: Flow and the Psychology of Discovery and Invention, (New York: Harper Perennial,1997) , 10.

36. The Office of Foreign Disaster Assistance is responsible for Relief while the USAID responsible for Development.

37. 1The President of the United States, National Security Presidential Directive/NSPD-44 (7 December 2005), 2.

38. Department of Defense, Directive Number 3000.5, 28 November 2005, 2.

39. Sarah Sewall "Modernizing U.S. Counterinsurgency: Rethinking Risk and Developing a National Strategy," Military Review, (2006) 109.

40. Sarah Sewall. Introduction. The U.S. Army/Marine Corps Counterinsurgency Field Manual. By General David H. Petraeus, Lieutenant General James F. Amos, and Lieutenant Colonel John A. Nagl. Chicago: University of Chicago Press, 2007. xl.

41. The Quadrennial Diplomacy and Development Review, Department of State, Washington, DC, 2010. 122.

42. *Ibid.*

43. The Quadrennial Diplomacy and Development Review, Department of State, Washington, DC, 2010.124

44. *Ibid.*, 42.

45. *Ibid*, 43.

46. U.S. Joint Chiefs of Staff, Stability Operations, Joint Publication 3-07 (Washington, DC: U.S. Joint Chiefs of Staff, August 11, 2011), I-2.

47. The UK manual JDP 3-40, *Stabilisation: The Military Contribution* utilizes the Surge in Iraq as a case study on human security informed stability operations.

48. Gray, Colin: War, Peace and International Relations - An Introduction to Strategic History, (New York: Routledge, 2007), p. 154.

49. *Ibid*, pp.1, 186.

50. B.H. Liddell Hart, Strategy, (New York: Praeger, 1967), 335-336.

51. Csíkszentmihályi, Creativity: Flow and the Psychology of Discovery and Invention, 27.

52. *Ibid*, 28.

53. *Ibid*.

54. A Defense, Diplomacy, and Development Conference was held at the Elliott School of International Affairs, George Washignton University on March 26, 2011 entitled "Building America's Next Grand Strategy." Conference literature stated: "Grand strategy refers to the collection of plans and policies that comprise a state's deliberate effort to harness political, military, diplomatic, and economic tools to advance their national interest. For nearly two decades, the United States has lacked a continuing grand strategy, or an overarching vision of what America's diplomatic and military efforts should seek to achieve, to guide our international relations. There is no single explanation for our failure to build a lasting grand strategic vision, but perhaps the biggest reason — and the most troubling — is that our foreign policies now seem to reflect our domestic politics: divided, polarized, and stagnant."

55. James G. March, "Exploration and Exploitation in Organizational Learning." Organization Science 2, no. 1 (1991): 71.

56. Tobias von Gienanth, Peace Operations 2025, 13.

57. *Ibid*.

58. Marquis, Jefferson P. Developing an Army Strategy for Building Partner Capacity for Stability Operations. RAND Arroyo Center, 2010. xiii

www.ingramcontent.com/pod-product-compliance
Lightning Source LLC
Chambersburg PA
CBHW071132280526
45787CB00003B/1254